DINOMUMMY

THE LIFE, DEATH AND DISCOVERY OF DAKOTA, A DINOSAUR FROM HELL CREEK

DINOMUMMY

THE LIFE, DEATH AND DISCOVERY OF DAKOTA, A DINOSAUR FROM HELL CREEK

Dr Phillip Lars Manning

Foreword by Tyler Lyson

KINGFISHER

KINGFISHER

Edited by Hannah Wilson
Designed by Mike Davis
Cover design by Mike Buckley
Picture research by Cee Weston-Baker
Production by Nancy Roberts and Lindsey Scott
DTP by Catherine Hibbert and Nicky Studdart

Kingfisher Publications Plc
New Penderel House
283–288 High Holborn
London WC1V 7HZ
www.kingfisherpub.com
First published by Kingfisher Publications Plc 2007
10 9 8 7 6 5 4 3 2 1

1TR/0807/WRLDPRNT/SCHOY(SCHOY)/157MA/C

ISBN: 978 0 7534 1402 6

A CIP record for this book is available from the British Library.

Printed in China

*This book is dedicated to anyone who
has picked up a fossil and dreamt of
lost worlds and forgotten lives.*

Dr Phillip Lars Manning

Contents

Foreword

I have been passionate about dinosaurs ever since my oldest brother, Ryan, and I found the fossilized jaw of a duck-billed hadrosaur when I was six years old. The fossil, which I've still got in a shoebox in my bedroom, made me want to learn everything about hadrosaurs and all the other dinosaurs.

The fossil also made me realize that anyone can hunt for and find dinosaurs. At the age of six, I was too young to look for fossils by myself, but I was very determined. I managed to persuade my very patient and loving mother to drive me out to the remote Hell Creek badlands, which surround my home-town of Marmarth, South Dakota, USA. She would sit in a deckchair with one eye on her book and one eye on me as I dug about in the dirt, looking for more dinosaur bones.

As a teenager, my persistence and passion grew. With a fellow budding fossil expert, I set up the Marmarth Research Foundation, an organization devoted to the excavation, preservation and study of dinosaur fossils. The headquarters were in a garage, but that didn't hold us back – soon bones from *Triceratops*, *Pachycephalosaurus* and even *T. rex* were pouring in. But none of those finds came close to my discovery, aged 16, on a late summer evening while fossil-hunting on my uncle's ranch. I found Dakota, a mummified duck-billed dinosaur. A 'dinomummy' so rare and so special that it could change the way we think about dinosaurs.

Dinomummy is Dakota's story. It's an adventure through time as well as science. Enjoy the ride!

Tyler Lyson

Tyler Lyson, PhD student of palaeontology at Yale University, founder of the Marmarth Research Foundation and discoverer of Dakota

This is the hadrosaur jawbone that I found when I was six.

Life and death in Hell Creek

It is the age of the dinosaurs, a time when the largest creatures that ever lived walked the Earth. One of these strange reptiles, a hadrosaur, emerges from the ferns and lush plants that line the river. Sixty-five million years from now, he will be recognized as one of the most important dinosaurs ever found and he will be named Dakota. But today, stepping into the morning sun, unaware of his future, the animal thinks only of surviving another day in Hell Creek.

A large and heavy dinosaur, Dakota moves cautiously on
thick, muscular legs to reach the river's edge. The toes of
his padded feet spread wide to stop him sinking into the wet
sand and his tail sways gently to balance his long body. He is not
yet an adult, but already he is almost eight metres long, nearly the
length of a bus. Dakota drops onto slender forearms, ready to drink.

Suddenly, across the water, two male *Pachycephalosaurus* clash in a violent display of strength. Dakota watches as they charge at each other like battering rams, delivering powerful blows with their thick, domed skulls. Today, their aggressive head-butts are designed to impress females of their kind. On other days, they might be used in defence against predators.

Another plant-eater is quietly watching the contest. The three-horned *Triceratops* is better prepared for defending herself against the giant carnivores of Hell Creek. A heavy and powerful creature, about twice the size of a rhinoceros, she can cause severe damage with her two longest horns while remaining protected by her solid neck frill. Dakota has no such armour or weapons.

13

Dakota returns to the protection of his herd, which is grazing nearby. These gentle plant-eaters rely on safety in numbers. Young and vulnerable, Dakota buries himself in the centre of the group.

It is autumn and the hadrosaurs have just arrived in Hell Creek. Every year, they migrate from the north to escape its cool, dry winters. Hell Creek is warm and wet all year round and the herd has come to feed on its lush plant life.

A lone *Ankylosaurus*, slow and heavy under the weight of her armoured plates, joins the hadrosaurs. The movements of the dinosaurs do not go unnoticed. From the cover of nearby vegetation, a pack of *Saurornitholestes* quietly emerges. These vicious raptors are stalking the herd, waiting for the right moment to attack.

The *Saurornitholestes* have chosen their victim.
But this time, it is not Dakota or another
hadrosaur – it is the young *Ankylosaurus*.
The predators, intelligent and fast, circle the
dinosaur and snap at her with razor-sharp teeth.

16

As Dakota turns to flee, he sees one of the raptors leap
onto the animal's back and climb up it using its curved
claws as hooks. But the desperate attacker will struggle to
pierce the armoured plating of his prey. Then *Ankylosaurus*,
with a heavy blow from his large tail club, knocks aside
another *Saurornitholestes* like a skittle. The battle will be
long and hard. Dakota does not stay around to watch.

17

Later, some of Dakota's herd stop to eat. With strong mouths shaped like duck bills, they snap leaves and twigs from bushes and grind the food with their teeth. Others, including Dakota, choose to drink and, one by one, they drop onto all fours to suck up water. It has rained heavily recently and the river has burst its banks in places, creating useful watering holes. All the hadrosaurs remain alert, constantly listening and watching. Suddenly, Dakota looks up. Something large is crashing through the undergrowth.

And it is coming closer...

Tyrannosaurus rex! The herd begins to snort and shriek in terror. As the hadrosaurs struggle to turn and flee, they kick clouds of dust into the hot air. The giant predator surveys the scene slowly, looking for an easy victim. She spots a young adult on the far left of the herd. It's Dakota. Mouth bulging with teeth like steak knives, the tyrannosaur begins to stride through the water...

It is the end of the day. As the sun sets over Hell Creek, Dakota lies still and silent. He has not survived. Strangely, there are no signs of injury to his body. If he was killed by the *Tyrannosaurus rex*, why wasn't he torn to pieces? Why wasn't he eaten?

Millions and millions of years will pass before these questions find answers. Dakota's body will lie buried in Hell Creek while Earth's continents collide to form towering mountains, while ice ages come and go, and while humans take their very first footsteps.

But for now, for the dinosaurs of Hell Creek, *a new destruction is just around the corner...*

22

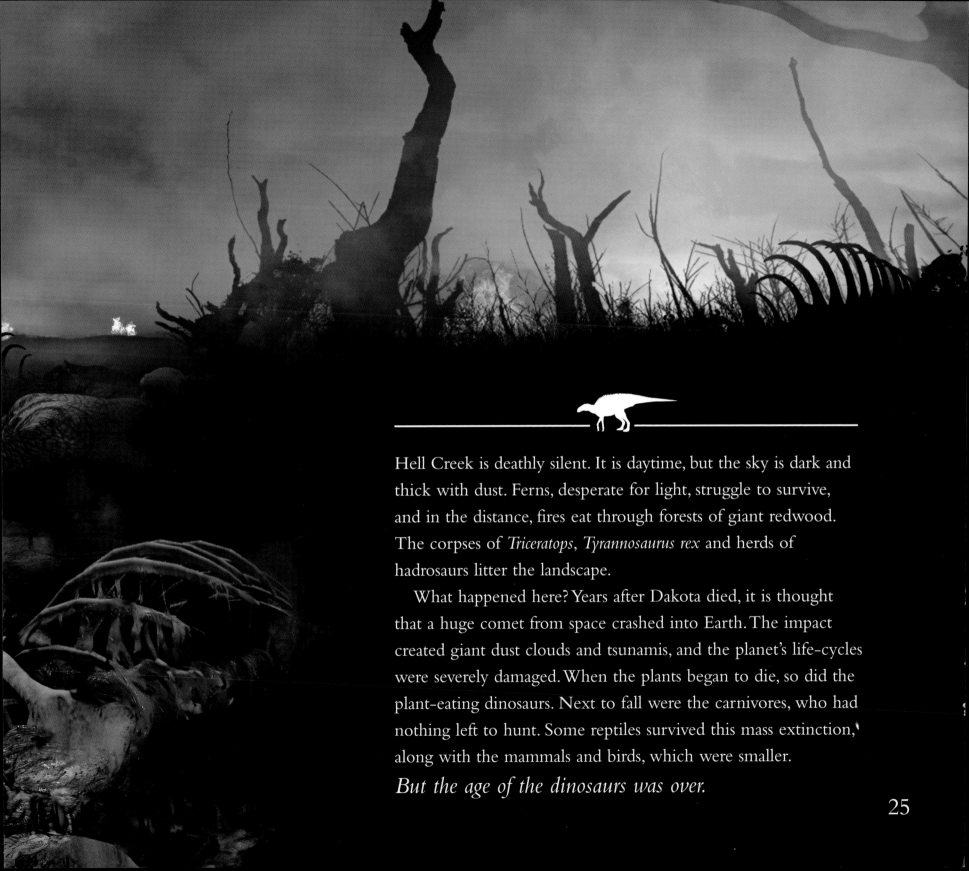

Hell Creek is deathly silent. It is daytime, but the sky is dark and thick with dust. Ferns, desperate for light, struggle to survive, and in the distance, fires eat through forests of giant redwood. The corpses of *Triceratops, Tyrannosaurus rex* and herds of hadrosaurs litter the landscape.

What happened here? Years after Dakota died, it is thought that a huge comet from space crashed into Earth. The impact created giant dust clouds and tsunamis, and the planet's life-cycles were severely damaged. When the plants began to die, so did the plant-eating dinosaurs. Next to fall were the carnivores, who had nothing left to hunt. Some reptiles survived this mass extinction, along with the mammals and birds, which were smaller.

But the age of the dinosaurs was over.

25

Digging for dinosaurs

A young man is walking through the remote, dusty hills of Hell Creek. Tyler keeps his eyes to the ground, looking for tiny splinters of bone among the crumbling rocks. He has hunted for dinosaurs in this way for as long as he can remember. The afternoon sun is fading and the straps of his rucksack are beginning to gnaw at his shoulders. It is time for him to go home – empty handed. But just as he is about to leave, Tyler finds something that will begin an incredible adventure and change his life forever. He finds Dakota.

Something has caught his eye. Tyler kneels down to brush away the stones and dirt that loosely cover it. A dinosaur bone! By its shape and size, he knows immediately that it is a vertebra, a tail or back bone. It probably belongs to the tail of a hadrosaur, a duck-billed, plant-eating dinosaur. As he sweeps away more of the soil, he finds another vertebra. Then another. Amazingly, the three 'verts' are articulated, which means that they are arranged in the correct order. The bones were not washed away in a river or moved about by a hungry scavenger.

It is getting dark now and the coyotes are beginning to howl. Tyler works quickly to collect the bones. Only two of them have fully 'weathered out', exposed by wind, rain and snow. Gently, he places the two verts in a sample bag and records the site's location with his GPS receiver. Then, switching on his torch, he begins the long walk back to his pick-up truck. Apart from the third, partly buried vert, he doesn't think there are any other bones left in the ground.

tail bones in
sample bag

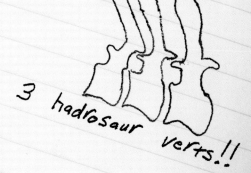

3 hadrosaur verts!!

It is many months later and Tyler has sent me an email. I am Dr Phil Manning, a palaeontologist at the University of Manchester in the UK. Like Tyler, I have loved dinosaurs since childhood. It all began when I was five years old. My parents took me to the Natural History Museum in London, and its enormous *Diplodocus* skeleton was the most amazing thing I had ever seen. My first find came a couple of years later when, in my own garden, I found a vertebra from an ichthyosaur, an ancient sea creature.

In his email, Tyler describes his own vertebra discovery in Hell Creek. He went back to the site to dig around the hadrosaur tail bone left in the ground. He discovered that it was connected to the rest of the tail! Then he uncovered something even more incredible, and his email included a photograph of it – dinosaur skin! Bumpy, scaly dinosaur skin!

Tyler had found a dinomummy!

A dinomummy is more than just a fossilized skeleton. It has some fossilized 'soft tissue' such as skin and possibly organs, too. No one knows exactly how dinomummies form as they are very rare. When an animal dies, its flesh normally rots away or is eaten by scavengers before it can fossilize.

Dinomummies are incredibly exciting. They can provide the chance to see what a dinosaur really looks like. Does it have spines on its head, scales down its back or bite-marks on its arm? Tyler is not sure how much of his dinosaur is mummified yet, but I want to help him find out. I book the next flight to North Dakota, USA. I am going to Hell Creek.

After a long, long journey, I arrive in Marmarth, Tyler's home-town. It's great to meet Tyler, but there is no time to waste – we jump into my pick-up truck and head out into the badlands.

About an hour later, there we are, on a hill overlooking Tyler's dig site. This is the ultimate dinosaur territory – the amazing Hell Creek Formation, a series of rock layers hundreds of kilometres wide and almost a kilometre deep. This layer is the tomb of the very last dinosaurs that lived on Earth. *Triceratops*, *Pachycephalosaurus* and one of the greatest predators of all time, *Tyrannosaurus rex*. As Tyler and I look out over this ancient landscape, we try to imagine the vast herds of hadrosaurs that grazed here in prehistoric times.

The body of one of them lies before us now, most of it still buried. The bones found so far are articulated and the fossilized skin is in excellent condition, so Tyler believes that the rest of the dinosaur is there, in the ground. But we will not know for sure until we begin a full excavation. We will need to gather scientists for every stage of the dig: geochemists to study the rocks and soil; palaeobotanists to look for ancient plant life; mapping experts to chart the shape of the land; and plenty of volunteers to dig up rock. No stone will be left unturned – literally!

A few weeks later, a team of scientists and volunteers gather at the site. Armed with picks and spades, we start to dig away the 'overburden', the tonnes and tonnes of soil around the tail bones. For the moment, we have to leave some rock, called the matrix, around the dinomummy to protect it. So, we stop digging when we hit a red-coloured layer as this means we are getting close to the fossilized skin.

Bit by bit, little by little, a shape begins to appear from the ground – the outline of a dinosaur! Although the matrix still hides much of the detail, it looks as if our dinomummy is complete!

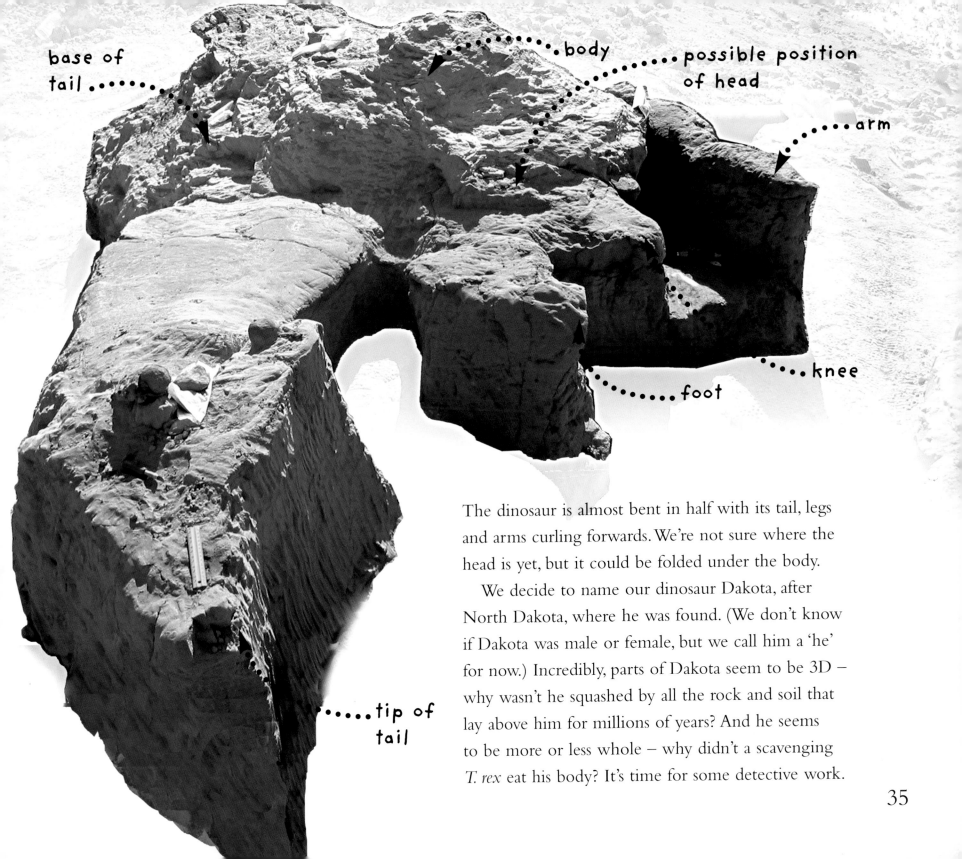

base of
tail

body

possible position
of head

arm

knee

foot

tip of
tail

The dinosaur is almost bent in half with its tail, legs
and arms curling forwards. We're not sure where the
head is yet, but it could be folded under the body.

We decide to name our dinosaur Dakota, after
North Dakota, where he was found. (We don't know
if Dakota was male or female, but we call him a 'he'
for now.) Incredibly, parts of Dakota seem to be 3D –
why wasn't he squashed by all the rock and soil that
lay above him for millions of years? And he seems
to be more or less whole – why didn't a scavenging
T. rex eat his body? It's time for some detective work.

Dinosaur excavations are all about rocks. Dakota has slowly turned to stone, having fossilized over millions of years, and he is buried in rock. I dig a trench nearby to have a look at the different layers. This area is made up of soft mudstones and sandstones, which might explain why his body was not crushed. I take samples of rock at the same level as Dakota's body and from levels above and below. The rock below Dakota is older than the dinosaur, and the rock above is younger.

Near the bottom of my trench, I notice a strange yellow sulphur ring, which may indicate a decaying plant or animal. As Dakota decayed and fossilized, he also changed the surrounding rock. So, when they are studied later, my rock samples may tell us something about what happened to Dakota.

.......sulphur ring

rock samples..........

36

camera

LIDAR
laser
scanner

On a nearby hill, a 'LIDAR' machine is busily shooting out lasers to different points on the landscape and examining how they bounce back. It uses this information to create a 3D map. Sitting down with my laptop computer, I have a look at a rough version of the map. Today's rock layers can tell us what the land was like in prehistoric times, and it seems as if Dakota is lying at the edge of an ancient river. Now it is starting to make sense! Perhaps the dinosaur's body was buried quickly in wet sand before a *T. rex* had time to munch it up! And the water from the river probably helped the chemical process that mummified Dakota. But does the river explain how the dinosaur died?

Did Dakota drown?

3D map

While I discuss dino life and death with Tyler, scientists Professor Rob Gawthorpe and Dr Kevin Taylor uncover something interesting – cement. Not the cement that holds houses together, but the natural sort that holds rocks together. This reddish brown rock (siderite) encased the dinosaur in a rocky coat of armour, cementing the mudstone and sandstone together. Without it, Dakota would have disintegrated millions of years ago.

Soon afterwards, Tyler finds a fossilized leaf. It is the same age as Dakota and the rest of the Hell Creek Formation – 65 to 67 million years old. Is the leaf another clue? The leaf belonged to a flowering tree like a modern sycamore. Today, there are no trees, but prehistoric Hell Creek was bursting with lush, green vegetation. When plants rot away, they affect the chemicals in the soil. And it was the chemistry of the ground that preserved Dakota so beautifully. Tyler's leaf is another clue because, in some small way, it helped turn Dakota into a dinomummy.

sycamore tree

Tyler's fossilized leaf

siderite ....

39

After many long, hard days, the dig is over. It is time to pack up our bags and leave Hell Creek. There's just one problem – we have to pack up an enormous, 10-tonne dinosaur, too. To stop moisture seeping into the matrix, we cover Dakota with tin foil until he looks like a giant turkey ready for the oven! Then Tyler dips strips of sackcloth into buckets of thick, white plaster of Paris and lays them over the dinomummy. The plaster will set to form a hard, protective covering called a field jacket. Tyler and the team must work quickly because the plaster dries rapidly in the hot sun.

As we cover our mummy in plaster, it gets bigger and bigger and heavier and heavier. No digger will be able to lift it! Luckily, we find a natural break at the base of Dakota's tail. After days of carefully cutting and digging along the break, the tail is gone, leaving two, more manageable chunks of dinosaur. Then we drill under the body block so that we can insert a metal support frame beneath it.

•.Dakota's tail was carefully removed from here.

41

Finally, both the tail and the body are lying on metal frames, encased in their tough, white field jackets. As Tyler and I wait for the digger to arrive, we look at the enormous three-tonne tail block. We are proud of Dakota's tail – it is the first mummified hadrosaur tail ever found. And it looks as if the skin and flesh of the tail extend beyond the last vertebra. This would mean that hadrosaur tails were longer than scientists currently think they were. We will not be able to confirm this until we examine the dinomummy properly, but Tyler and I are sure that *Dakota is going to rewrite hadrosaur history!*

tip of skin?

tip of tail bones

A deep rumbling noise fills the air and the digger chugs slowly over the hill. Nervously, we watch as it begins to scoop the body block into its bucket. For one nail-biting moment, the block wobbles on the edge of the bucket. If the digger drops the dinosaur, not even its field jacket will save Dakota from being smashed to pieces. But the digger safely delivers its precious load to a nearby lorry. The dinosaur is about to begin a long, bumpy journey to the science lab.

After more than 65 million years, Dakota is leaving Hell Creek.

Secrets from the grave

In a dark, dusty laboratory, Dakota has begun to emerge from his rocky armour. Several weeks have passed since the dinosaur bumped and juddered away from the wilderness of Hell Creek to the cool quiet of the lab. When the dinosaur arrived, we began work on the tail block first, cutting away its field jacket with circular saws. Now we pick up smaller tools to begin the 'preparation' work. We scrape away the tail's protective rock matrix. As we work, we take more soil samples, wrapping them in plastic and stacking them on the section from which they came. The process is slow and painstaking, but the goal is simple – to remove as much of the encasing rock as possible. We want to leave nothing but dinosaur.

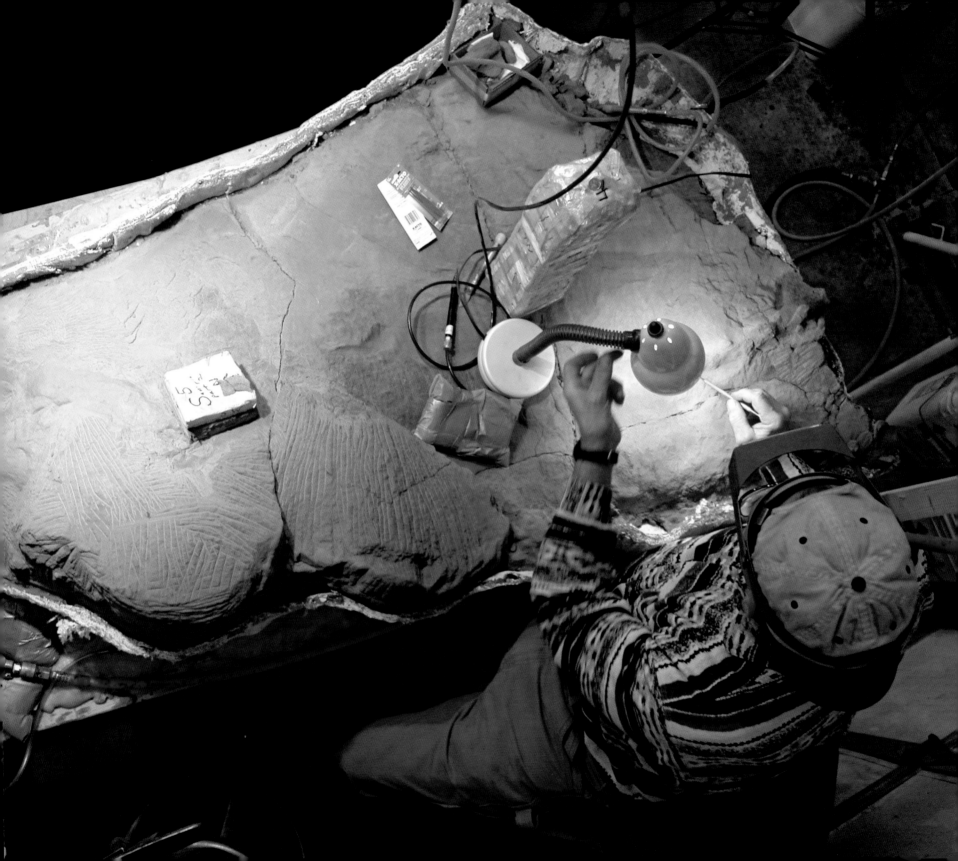

Tyler begins preparation work on one of Dakota's feet, which was carefully separated from the body block during the dig. The dinosaur's fossilized skin is almost the same colour and texture as the surrounding rock and Tyler needs great skill to make sure that he does not chip away any of Dakota's stony flesh. Helped by a strong light and a magnifying glass, he uses a dental pick to remove the matrix, grain by grain. It will take a team of preparators many, many months to finish the foot, but already skin scales are beginning to emerge.

Smaller scales
at elbow allow
skin to flex.

Changes in scale size
may indicate changes
in colour.

extra, smaller
digit for
grasping
branches

glove of skin
between fingers

scute

Similar prep work is carried out on Dakota's left arm and hand. He had three main fingers and, like his toes, they were enveloped in a 'glove' of skin, which created a wide surface area and prevented him from sinking into wet mud. The quality of Dakota's skin preservation is outstanding and we uncover scales that vary in size and shape. There seem to be smaller scales near the joints. These probably allowed the skin to flex as the elbow or wrist bent. Along the tail, differences in the scales are also appearing. Large toughened scutes – plates embedded in the skin like those on a crocodile's back – are rising up out of the rock. These helped to protect the dinosaur's back from low-hanging branches – or from *T. rex* bites! Our study of Dakota is helping us to create a skin map for all hadrosaurs, detailing which types of scale covered which parts of the body.

tail vertebrae

Hadrosaur hipbones resemble those of modern birds.

a muscle that moves the leg

The ischium supports muscles and organs.

femur (thigh bone)

Widely spaced toes support body weighing more than 3 tonnes.

We do not want to dig into Dakota's skin, but we do need to examine his skeleton. We start by studying the few bones that are exposed – remember those tail vertebrae that Tyler found all those months ago? Those bones tell us that it is very likely that Dakota is an *Edmontosaurus annectens*, a species of hadrosaur common in Hell Creek. The length of Dakota's tail and arm suggest that Dakota is a juvenile, so we use the skeleton of another young dinosaur of this species to create a computer model of Dakota.

Using measurements from the 'skin envelope' (the skin that covers Dakota's body), we try to work out what might be inside the dinosaur, starting with the leg muscles. For the first time in hadrosaur history, we can make accurate calculations about how Dakota moved. The results show that Dakota, large and heavy though he was, could run!

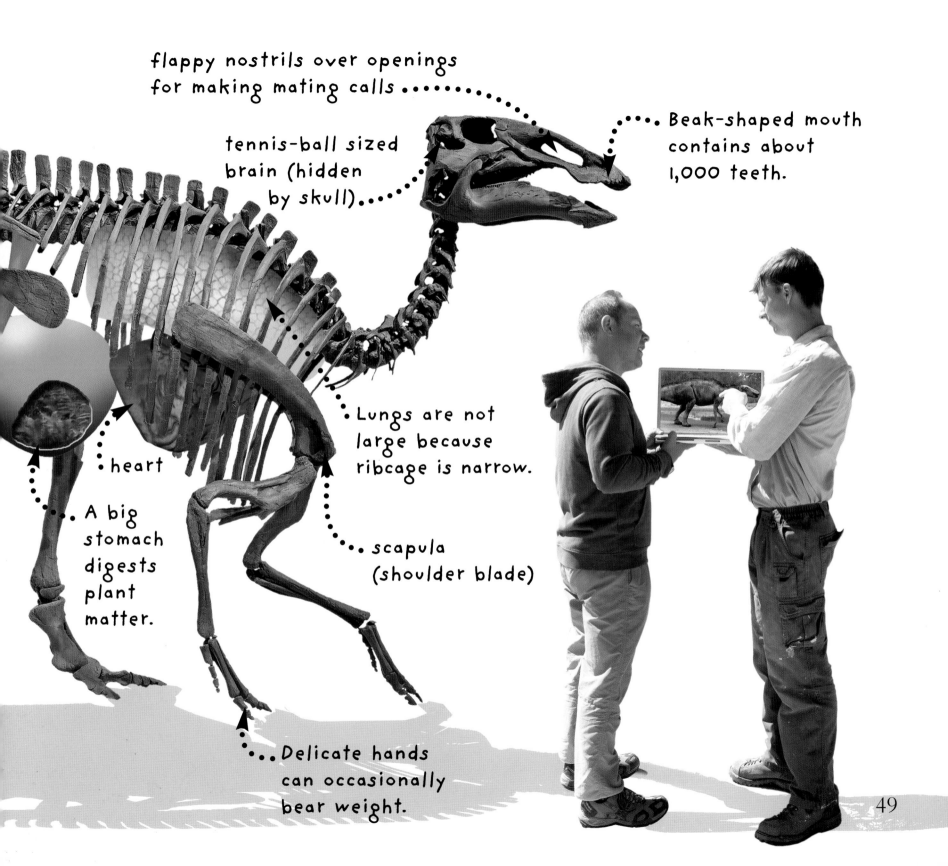

flappy nostrils over openings
for making mating calls ·······

tennis-ball sized
brain (hidden
by skull)·······

Beak-shaped mouth
contains about
1,000 teeth.

Lungs are not
large because
ribcage is narrow.

heart

A big
stomach
digests
plant
matter.

scapula
(shoulder blade)

Delicate hands
can occasionally
bear weight.

Remember those rock samples that I collected during the dig? Well, it's time to study those as well as samples taken during the prep work and from underneath Dakota's body. When the digger lifted away Dakota, the ground beneath him was stained a dark red colour. Dinosaur blood? No – the stain was caused by other fluids seeping out of his body after death.

I grind the rock into a fine powder and press it into a disc-shaped pellet. The pellet is put inside a huge X-ray machine that detects chemicals. The tests tell us that there were weak acids present. The acids were probably produced by Hell Creek's wet climate and lush vegetation – including Tyler's leaf! The acids helped to form the siderite that Rob and Kevin found. It is this siderite that encased Dakota, protecting him for so many millions of years.

I'm using a mini pestle and mortar to grind the rock.

This is a tiny piece of fossilized dinomummy!

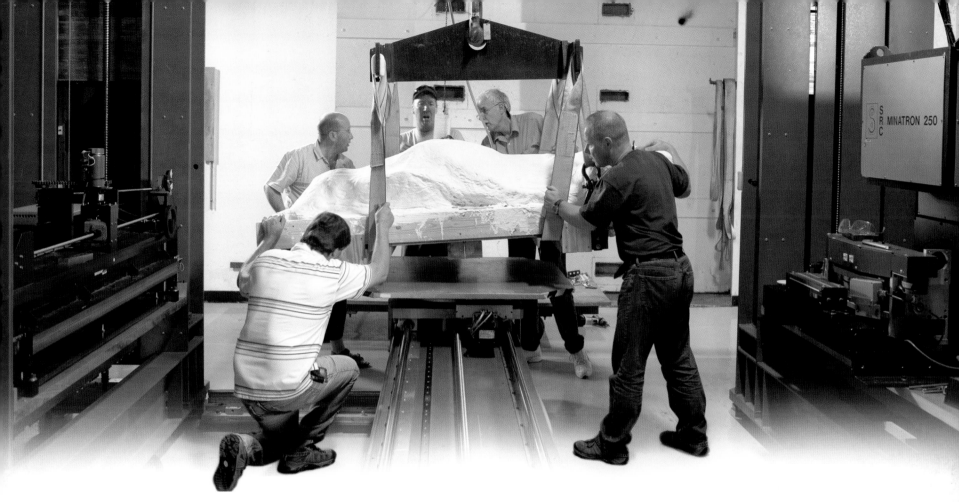

A few weeks later, Dakota is on the move again, plastered in a new field jacket to protect him during the journey. We're taking the dinosaur to California, to a scanning facility normally used to check space-shuttle parts for cracks. When we arrive, we carefully lower the dinosaur onto a sliding platform. The platform will move the block into the scanner, where X-ray beams will take a series of images from different angles.

When we scan the tail, we discover something pretty special – it *does* extend beyond the last vertebra. Tyler and I were right! Hadrosaur tails are longer than scientists previously thought! And this might be true of many other dinosaurs, so our discovery is very important for palaeontology.

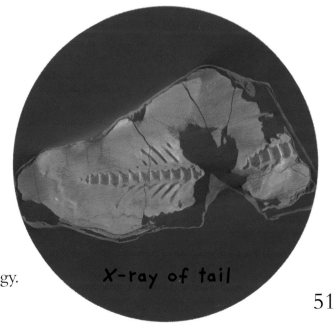

X-ray of tail

Back at our lab, prep work on the arm is finished. We have found something that has been seen only once before – a single fleshy pad on the palm. And, surprisingly, there are no hoof-like fingernails. This confirms that hadrosaurs did not permanently walk on all fours – their hands were not tough enough for the job.

The foot that Tyler is preparing, however, does have hooves. Hadrosaur hooves were made of keratin, like your fingernails are. Keratin is much tougher than skin, and Dakota's hooves are so well preserved that some of their keratin may not have turned to stone but survived! This is very, very rare and hugely exciting. It will tell us so much about what hadrosaurs are made of.

As we work on the body block, a few bones begin to emerge. This is strange – why isn't the chest area fully mummified?

body block

ribcage

shoulder blade

skin completely surrounds arm

hand

close-up of hand shows fleshy pad of palm

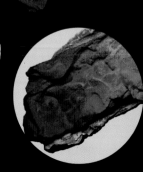

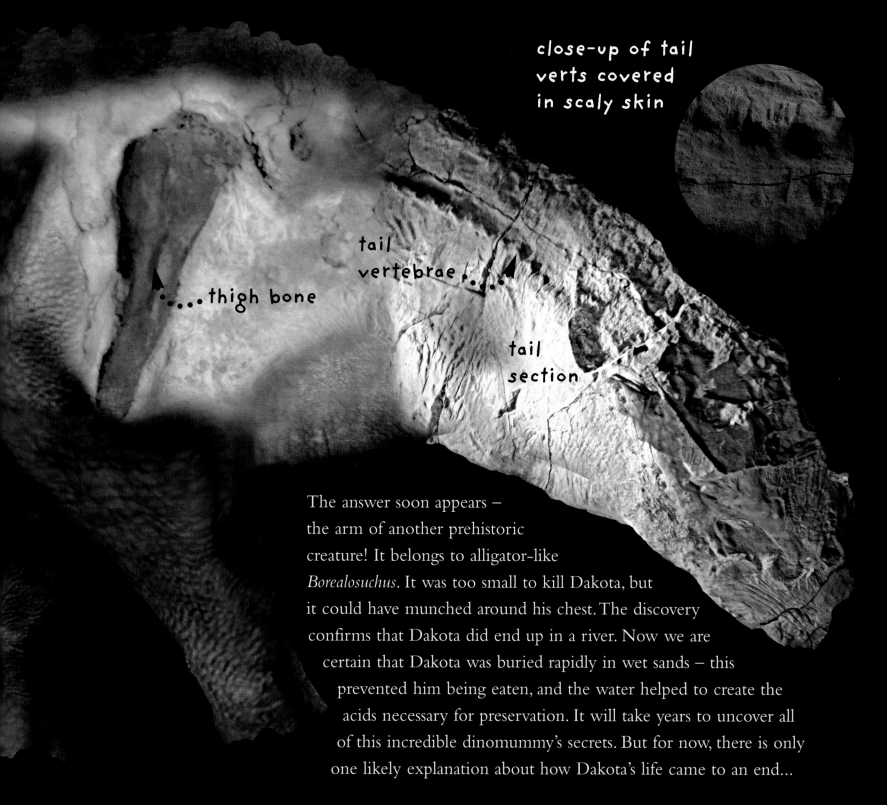

close-up of tail
verts covered
in scaly skin

tail
vertebrae

thigh bone

tail
section

The answer soon appears –
the arm of another prehistoric
creature! It belongs to alligator-like
Borealosuchus. It was too small to kill Dakota, but
it could have munched around his chest. The discovery
confirms that Dakota did end up in a river. Now we are
certain that Dakota was buried rapidly in wet sands – this
prevented him being eaten, and the water helped to create the
acids necessary for preservation. It will take years to uncover all
of this incredible dinomummy's secrets. But for now, there is only
one likely explanation about how Dakota's life came to an end...

As night falls, Dakota's body lies in the muddy shallows of a river. His body is twisted and crumpled, battered by the river that delivered him there. Earlier, when the *T. rex* charged into the herd of hadrosaurs, Dakota fled in terror and in his panic, he stumbled into the swollen river. Floodwaters were sweeping through Hell Creek and they quickly knocked the dinosaur off his feet. The river washed Dakota away from the jaws of the *T. rex*, but they also overpowered him. Dakota drowned.

Now his body has come to a rest in a bend of the river, where the current is gentle. A pack of scavenging *Borealosuchus* surrounds Dakota and dark blood seeps out of him, staining the water. Dakota is sinking quickly into the wet sands and soon only his chest will be exposed to the predators. In less than an hour, Dakota will slip out of sight.

Triassic

Earth has only one supercontinent, Pangaea.

Long-tailed pterosaur **Eudimorphodon** hunted fish.

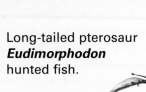

Meat-eating dinosaur **Coelophysis** both hunted live prey and scavenged for dead animals.

Mammal-like reptile **Lystrosaurus** had two tusks.

Tiny **Lagosuchus** had legs similar to those of its later relatives, the dinosaurs.

Many scientists think turkey-sized predator **Eoraptor** was the world's first dinosaur!

Mixosaurus, a marine reptile, not a dinosaur, had a long tail and paddle-like limbs.

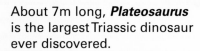

About 7m long, **Plateosaurus** is the largest Triassic dinosaur ever discovered.

The age of the dinosaurs

The dinosaurs of the Hell Creek Formation lived 65 to 67 million years ago, at the end of the Cretaceous Period. Dinosaurs have been around for about 230 million years, developing and changing during the Triassic, Jurassic and Cretaceous periods. Alongside the dinosaurs, giant reptiles swam in the seas and soared through the skies.

Jurassic

Pangaea begins to break into separate continents.

Dimorphodon, a pterosaur, had a large toothed beak.

Lesothosaurus, from modern-day South Africa, could run quickly on two legs.

Apatosaurus, a plant-eating giant, weighed about the same as four African elephants!

Megalosaurus was a powerful meat-eating predator.

Dilophosaurus had two crests on its head that were probably used to attract mates.

Plant-eating **Stegosaurus** had two rows of plates along its back.

Huayangosaurus, an older relative of *Stegosaurus*, was covered in protective spikes.

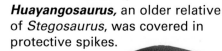

Plesiosaurus was a long-necked marine reptile.

Diplodocus was about the length of three double-decker buses!

Earth's land masses slowly move to today's positions.

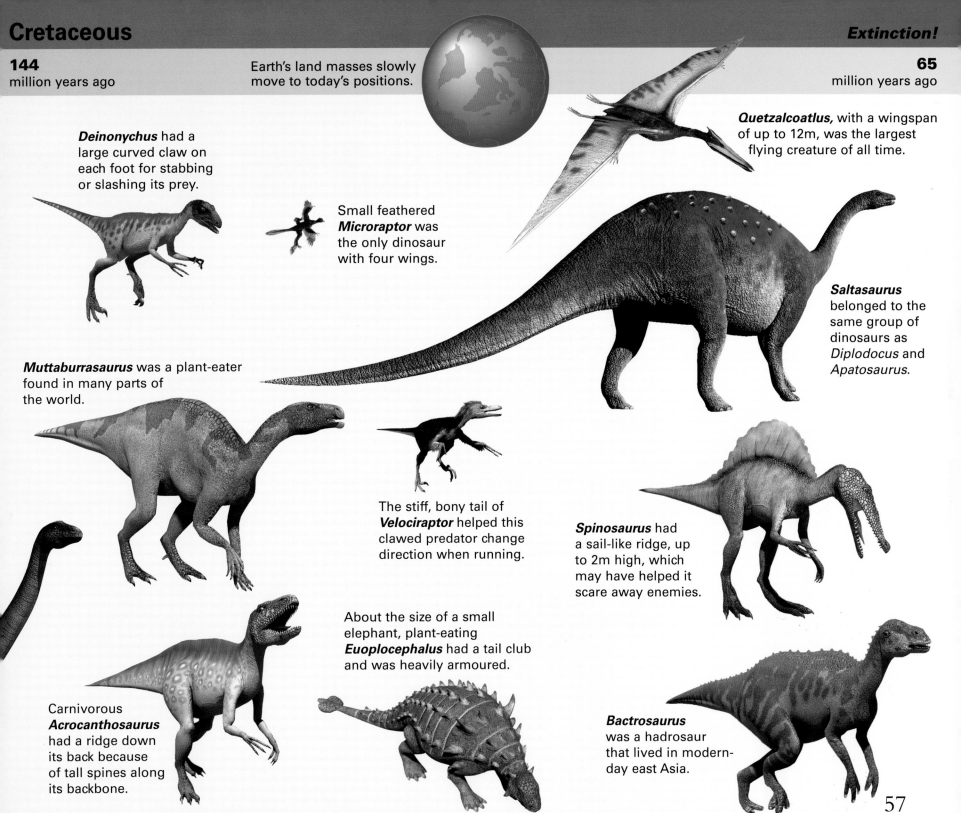

Quetzalcoatlus, with a wingspan of up to 12m, was the largest flying creature of all time.

Deinonychus had a large curved claw on each foot for stabbing or slashing its prey.

Small feathered **Microraptor** was the only dinosaur with four wings.

Saltasaurus belonged to the same group of dinosaurs as *Diplodocus* and *Apatosaurus.*

Muttaburrasaurus was a plant-eater found in many parts of the world.

The stiff, bony tail of **Velociraptor** helped this clawed predator change direction when running.

Spinosaurus had a sail-like ridge, up to 2m high, which may have helped it scare away enemies.

About the size of a small elephant, plant-eating **Euoplocephalus** had a tail club and was heavily armoured.

Carnivorous **Acrocanthosaurus** had a ridge down its back because of tall spines along its backbone.

Bactrosaurus was a hadrosaur that lived in modern-day east Asia.

57

Who's who in Hell Creek?

Many dinosaurs, reptiles, mammals and birds lived in and alongside the rivers of Hell Creek. Some fed on the seeds and leaves of plants and trees; others preyed on smaller animals. If the dinosaurs of Hell Creek could speak, and if Tyler and I could go back in time to interview them, food would probably be a hot topic. Teeth and claws helped predators to hunt, and armour-plating and horns helped plant-eaters avoid ending up on someone else's menu!

Ankylosaurus

What does your name mean? 'stiffened-lizard'

How big are you? About 9m long and 2m high. I weigh a hefty 4,500kg.

Meat or veg? Veg, please! I'm a herbivore.

Does anything eat you? My armour plating puts off most predators, but occasionally I get hassled by desperate meat-eaters.

You look quite weird. Yes, I look like I'm suffering from a bad case of warts! It's the lumpy, bony plates in my skin. My head is very big, too. My skull is a big bony block protecting my tiny brain.

Tell me something interesting. I love clubbing in the Cretaceous! The bone at the tip of my tail has expanded into a club. Any predators who want a piece of me have to watch out for my bone-crushing tail blows!

Avisaurus

What does your name mean? 'bird-lizard'

How big are you? My wingspan is about 1m.

Meat or veg? I eat meat, like one of your modern birds of prey. I hunt insects and small mammals, lizards and birds.

Whose menu are you on? I can fly away from most trouble, but if a large pterosaur is flying over Hell Creek, it might give me a hard time.

You look a bit like a modern bird (yawn). Wake up, please! Did you know that I have evolved from the meat-eating dinosaurs? And modern birds are my descendants. This means that the sparrows in your garden are distant relatives of the dinosaurs!

Borealosuchus

What does your name mean? 'northern-crocodile' (more or less)

How big are you? A little smaller than a modern croc – about 4.5m long and 300kg in weight.

Meat or veg? I eat turtles, fish and any mammals foolish enough to drink near to where I'm wallowing in the river.

Are you prey or a predator? Weren't you listening? I'm a predator, of course! But I'm also a scavenger, which means that I eat dead animals.

What's interesting about you? My family hasn't changed much in more than 100 million years – that's what's interesting about me! And that's because we survived when those wimpy dinosaurs died out!

Didelphodon

What does your name mean? 'opossum tooth' (an opossum is a small mammal)

How big are you? About the size of a badger – 50 to 100cm long. And I weigh about 10 to 20kg.

Meat or veg? Lizards, insects, bugs and a few juicy plants, please.

Does anything eat you? I'm too small for *T. rex* to spot, but, unfortunately for me, *Saurornitholestes* has got excellent eyesight...

Tell me something interesting. I'm a marsupial, like a kangaroo. Yup, I rear my babies in a pouch!

Edmontosaurus

What does your name mean? 'Edmonton-lizard' (I was first found near Edmonton in Canada)

How big are you? Very! Up to 12m long, 3m high and 3,500kg in weight.

Meat or veg? Plants, please.

Prey or predator? I prey on plants, but *T. rex* preys on me. Gulp!

Why do you look so strange? For a dinosaur, I don't look that weird, do I? I don't have strange spikes or horns. Perhaps my mouth looks a little odd to you. I am a hadrosaur and we 'duck-billed' dinosaurs have mouths shaped like beaks. Other members of the hadrosaur family look much more weird than me. They have strange head-crests and inflatable nose pouches!

Eubaena

What does your name mean? 'good turtle'

How big are you? I'm quite small really, about 30 to 50cm long. I'm a lightweight 3 to 5kg.

Meat or veg? I'll eat anything that will fit in my mouth – fish, bugs, plants... I'm pretty adaptable, which is one of the reasons why I survived when the dinosaurs died out.

Does anything eat you? *Borealosuchus* would like to crunch up my shell like a cream cracker if it got the chance...

You're just a turtle. What's interesting about you? Don't you think it is interesting that turtles have lived for more than 200 million years? Humans haven't even been around for one million years!

Ornithomimus

What does your name mean? 'bird mimic' (I'm a bit like a bird in some ways)

How big are you? About 4.5m long, 2.5m high and 500kg in weight.

Meat or veg? Good question! I'm toothless so I love soft fruits. But I never say no to a mouthful of mammal or lizard. I'm not fussy!

Does anything eat you? Only if it can catch me! I'm possibly one of the fastest of all the dinosaurs. My long legs help me run at speeds of about 50km/h.

You remind me of something... Is it an ostrich? My body shape is similar to an ostrich's. Imagine me covered in feathers.

Tell me something interesting. My bones are hollow, so I'm pretty light. This helps me to run quickly.

Pachycephalosaurus

What does your name mean? 'thick-headed lizard' (don't laugh!)

How big are you? About 4.6m long, 1.5m high and 1,000kg in weight.

Meat or veg? My teeth are excellent at shredding plants. They're not adapted for chewing meat.

Are you on anyone's menu? I'm good at headbutting. That usually keeps me out of trouble.

What's happening with the dome head? The top of my skull is 25cm thick – excellent for headbutting my male buddies. This usually impresses the ladies!

Saurornitholestes

What does your name mean? 'lizard-bird thief'

How big are you? Not very – about 1.80m long, 0.9m tall. I weigh about 40kg.

Meat or veg? Just meat – reptile or mammal will do.

Prey or predator? I'm a predator and a super-fast one – just look at the length of my legs!

You look a bit like *Velociraptor*. That's my cousin! We've both got a long, curved claw on our second toe. Perfect for ripping apart prey.

What's interesting about you? I'm a bit of a mystery. You humans know very little about me. In Hell Creek, you've found only pieces of my skull.

Stegoceras

What does your name mean? 'roofed horn'

How big are you? About 2m long, 1m tall and 50kg in weight.

Meat or veg? Plants, please. I'm a strict vegetarian.

Whose menu are you on? As a small plant-eater, I'm on quite a few of the meat-eaters' menus, unfortunately.

You look like *Pachycephalosaurus*. Well spotted. I'm a smaller relative. We've both got thickened skulls for using as battering rams.

Tell me something interesting. My neck vertebrae prevent my head from twisting when I am doing a spot of headbutting.

Thescelosaurus

What does your name mean? 'marvellous lizard'

How big are you? About 3.9m long, 0.9m high and only 100kg in weight.

Meat or veg? I'm a herbivore – so veg, please.

Prey or predator? Prey, unfortunately...

You look a bit boring. Why don't you have horns or armour plating? I don't need them because I don't stay around to fight. I'm a speed machine – I run away on my muscular, long legs.

Torosaurus

What does your name mean? 'pierced lizard' (the bone inside my head crest is pierced with holes)

How big are you? About 6.2m long, 2.4m high. At almost 7,500kg in weight, I'm the heaviest resident of Hell Creek (my neck frill weighs a lot).

Meat or veg? Veg, please, and lots of it. I need to eat a lot to provide energy for my large, bulky body.

Prey or predator? Prey, if anyone can get past my 1m-long horns.

You look a bit like Triceratops. We're related. We're both ceratopsians, which means we have mouths like parrot beaks and many of us have horns and neck frills.

Triceratops

What does your name mean? 'three-horned face'

How big are you? About 8m long, 3m high and a hefty 6,000kg in weight.

Meat or veg? Veg. I'm a herbivore.

Prey or predator? Alas, I'm prey, but with my weight and horns, I'm no packed lunch!

Why do you look so weird? My head is huge. And I've got three long horns that I use to fight other *Triceratops* and to protect my family.

Tell me something interesting. My neck frill is solid bone – my ceratopsian relatives have holes in theirs.

Tyrannosaurus rex

What does your name mean? 'tyrant-lizard king' – in other words, I'm the boss!

How big are you? Enormous! 12m long (some say longer), 4m high and 4,500kg in weight.

Meat or veg? *Triceratops* meat, *Edmontosaurus* meat, and any other meat I can get my teeth into. I don't bother with mammals – they're not even a mouthful.

Prey or predator? What do you think? I am Hell Creek's top predator.

Why do you look so weird? Maybe because my skull is nearly 2m long with teeth the size of bananas. And I have tiny arms. But I wouldn't call me weird if I were you...

Glossary

acid
a strong substance that can dissolve things

articulated
arranged in the original position of the skeleton

badlands
an area of wilderness with a dry climate, little vegetation and soft ground that has been shaped by wind and rain into hills

carnivore
a meat-eater

ceratopsian
one of a group of plant-eating dinosaurs with beaked mouths. Some, such as *Triceratops*, had horns and a neck frill.

chemical
a substance with specific characteristics

comet
a ball of rock, dust and ice, often with a 'tail' of gas and dust, that circles the Sun

continent
a large land mass on Earth

coyote
a wild animal that is native to North America and is a relative of the wolf

digit
a finger or a toe

dinomummy
a dinosaur whose fossilized remains include some soft tissue, such as skin, as well as the skeleton

dinosaur
a prehistoric reptile that lived between about 230 and 65 million years ago. *Dinosaur* means 'terrible lizard'.

evolve
to change gradually

excavation
the careful removal of a fossil from the ground and the recording of this process

extinction
the dying out of a species or group of animals all over the world

field jacket
a layer of tin foil covered in plaster-coated strips of sackcloth. It immobilizes and protects a dinosaur skeleton in the same way that a plaster cast protects a broken limb.

fossil
animal remains that have mineralized (turned to stone)

fossilization
the slow change of an animal as it becomes a fossil over millions of years

frill
the protective bony shield (part of the skull) that dinosaurs such as *Triceratops* have

GPS receiver
a Global Positioning System receiver calculates the exact position of its user with information sent by satellites

hadrosaur
a medium-sized plant-eating dinosaur with a mouth shaped like a duck's bill

Hell Creek Formation
a layer of clays, mudstones and sandstones that crosses the US states of Montana, North Dakota, South Dakota, and Wyoming. The rock was deposited during the end of the Late Cretaceous Period, burying dinosaurs of that age.

ice age
a period when extensive ice sheets spread over parts of Earth

icthyosaur
a marine reptile. *Ichthyosaur* means 'fish lizard'.

keratin	the tough material of fingernails	**raptor**	a slang term for a small, carnivorous dinosaur that walks on two legs
LIDAR	LIght Detection And Range technology uses light to pinpoint a 3D location	**reptile**	a 'cold-blooded', furless animal. Many reptile species lay eggs.
mammal	a warm-blooded, furry animal that produces milk to feed its young	**scavenger**	an animal that does not hunt for food, eating the remains of dead animals instead
matrix	the rock immediately surrounding a dinosaur fossil	**scute**	a bony plate, similar to those along a crocodile's back, that grows within the skin layer
migration	the regular movement of a group of animals from one area to another to find food and water, or to search for mates	**siderite**	a type of rock that is rich in iron
mummified	the preserved state of the body of a person or animal due to special conditions	**skin envelope**	the outer layer of skin that encloses the skeleton and internal body parts
overburden	the large quantity of rock and soil that needs to be dug away to access a fossil	**soft tissue**	the parts of an animal that are not made of bone. Soft tissues include muscle, skin, organs and keratin.
palaeontologist	a scientist who studies the history of all life on Earth	**species**	a group of animals that share common physical characteristics
predator	an animal that hunts for food	**sulphur**	sulphuric acid, a soft yellow substance
prehistoric	relating to the time before humans lived	**tsunami**	a series of giant waves caused by earthquakes or volcanic eruptions
preparation	the careful removal of rock, using small tools, to reveal the bones or skin envelope of a dinosaur	**vertebra**	a single bone that connects with other vertebrae to form the backbone (including the tail) of an animal
preparator	someone who carries out preparation or 'prep' work	**weathering out**	the exposing of a fossil when the soil that covers it is worn away by harsh weather conditions such as heavy rain
preservation	the condition of a specimen in terms of its decay or lack of decay. This is determined by how the animal died and was fossilized.	**X-ray**	a form of radiation (energy that moves in waves) that can help produce a picture of the inside of an object
pterosaur	one of a group of flying reptiles. *Pterosaur* means 'winged lizard'.		

Index

Acknowledgments

The Author wishes to thank: Tyler Lyson and the Marmarth Research Foundation and its team of volunteers; National Geographic Foundation (Research and Expedition) for grants that have supported the excavation, preparation and science; Boeing Corporation for access to their CT-scanning facility; Stephen Begin who has sacrificed so much of his time and eyesight preparing Dakota; Black Hills Institute of Geological Research, South Dakota; Prof. Kent Stevens at the University of Oregon; my colleagues at the University of Manchester and The Manchester Museum. And many thanks especially to Jo, Alice and Kate for allowing me vast quantities of time to explore a fascinating dinosaur called Dakota.

The Publisher would like to thank: Tyler Lyson; Neal Larson, Pete Larson, Bob Farrar and Larry Shaffer at the Black Hills Institute; Tony Cutting; Tim De Alwis; Simon Holland; Richard Platt

The Publisher would like to thank the following for permission to reproduce their material. Every care has been taken to trace copyright holders. However, if there have been unintentional omissions or failure to trace copyright holders, we apologize and will, if informed, endeavour to make corrections in any future edition.

Key: b = bottom, c = centre, l = left, r = right, t = top

Pages 1, 2-3, 4–5 Dean Steadman/Kingfisher Publications; 6 Phil Manning; 7 Dean Steadman/Kingfisher Publications; 8–9, 10–11, 12–13, 14–16, 16–17, 18–19, 20–21, 22–23, 24–25 Russell Gooday & Jon Hughes/Pixel Shack; 26–27, 28–29 Dean Steadman/Kingfisher Publications; 29br Pete Clayman; 30 Hannah Wilson; 31 Dean Steadman/Kingfisher Publications; 32–33 Dean Steadman/Kingfisher Publications (photographs); 32–33 Russell Gooday & Jon Hughes/Pixel Shack (digital artwork); 34 Dean Steadman/Kingfisher Publications & Tyler Lyson; 35 Tyler Lyson; 36–37, 38r–39 Dean Steadman/Kingfisher Publications; 38l Fritz Polking/Frank Lane Picture Agency; 40–41, 42 Dean Steadman/Kingfisher Publications; 43 National Geographic 2007; 44–45 National Geographic 2007; 46 Dean Steadman/Kingfisher Publications; 47 Russell Gooday & Jon Hughes/Pixel Shack; 48–49 Dean Steadman/Kingfisher Publications (with thanks to the Black Hills Institute for the skeleton); 50 Pete Clayman; 51 National Geographic 2007; 52cl, cb Tyler Lyson; 52–53, 53tr Black Hills Institute; 52–53 Russell Gooday & Jon Hughes/Pixel Shack (digital artwork); 54–55 Russell Gooday & Jon Hughes/Pixel Shack; 56–57 Steve Weston; 58bl Dean Steadman/Kingfisher Publications; 58–59 Russell Gooday & Jon Hughes/Pixel Shack except 58br, 59tr Steve Weston; 60–61 Russell Gooday & Jon Hughes/Pixel Shack except 60tl, 61bl Steve Weston; 62–63, 64 Dean Steadman/Kingfisher Publications